MW00901656

SIDEWAYS
THROUGH
ZION

SIDEWAYS THROUGH ZION

Richard Wells

EMBAJADORAS PRESS

Embajadoras Press
Ontario, Canada
www.embajadoraspress.com

Copyright © 2020 by Richard Wells
No part of this book may be used or reproduced
without permission of the author.

As in all things, love to Reggie Bardach —
for whom energy IS eternal delight

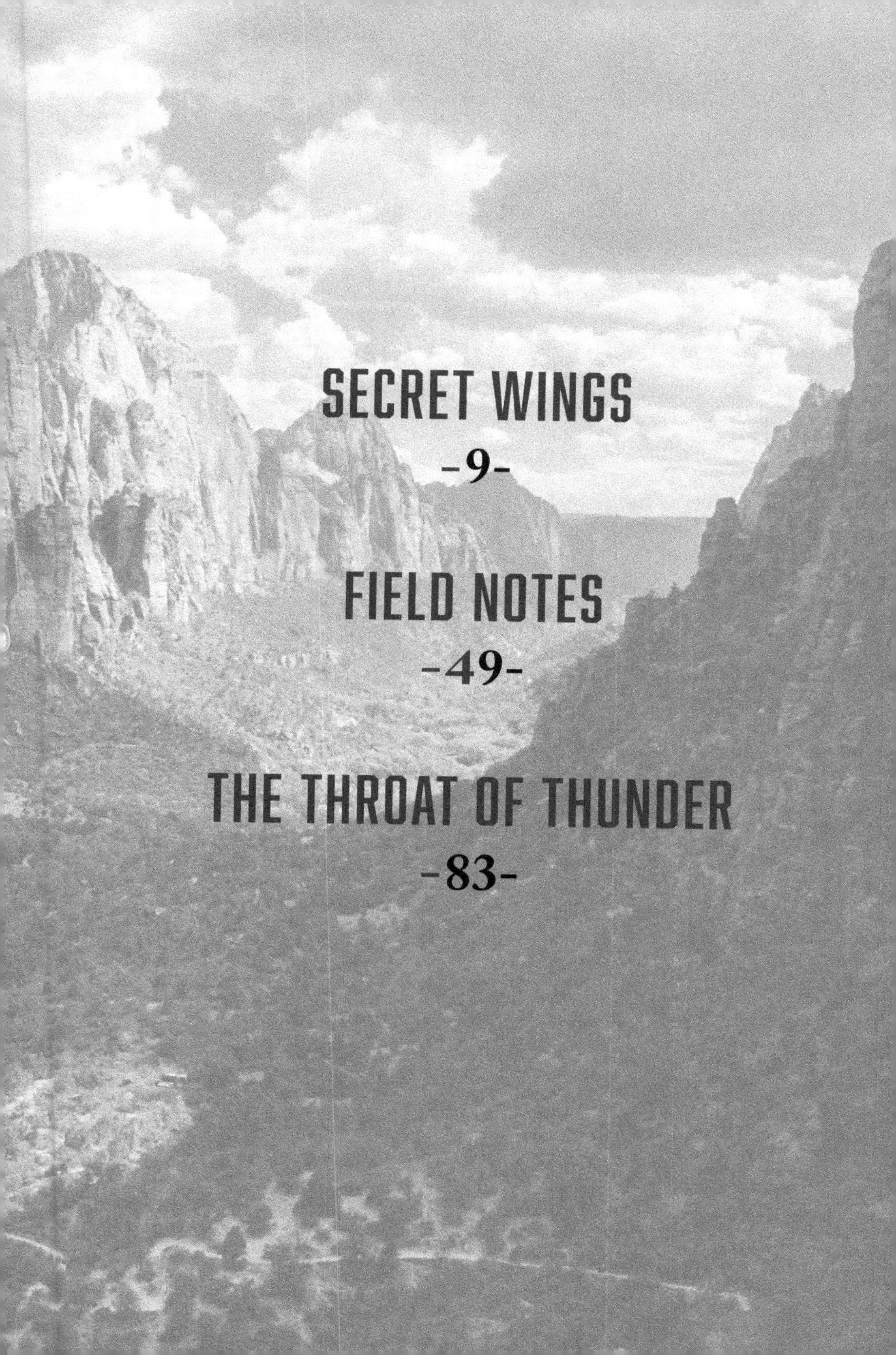

SECRET WINGS

Sacred Places

There are no paths
to sacred places —
only steps

One step
after another
until one day
you turn around
and there you are

A sacred place
unto yourself
and like no other.

I was five years old when I saw the garden.

My folks owned a cottage on about seven wooded acres in Northwestern Pennsylvania. It was a great place for a kid because there were a lot of opportunities to slip away and explore, and at five I didn't have to get very far to have an adventure. Sitting behind a tree, out of sight of the adults was enough to qualify, but one day, I slipped over the edged boundary of lawn and forest, and though I wasn't even out of shouting range I was in a different world — the darkened silence of woodland with sun dappling through treetops, no breeze, quiet defined by road noise outside the woods, and bird song within.

I walked a narrow path with woods to my right and a gully to my left; every step a little deeper into the mystery of being alone and away.

Eventually, the gully widened out, and at its widest point — changed. No longer a tangle of underbrush etched in grays and browns, but now soft with diffuse light, green of tall grass, spackled with the colors of wildflowers.

That wild garden was its own invitation, but an invitation I couldn't accept. The slope was just too steep and tangled. I sat on the edge, looking into the wonderland, and drawing some part of it into myself. Then I left, glad of my discovery, and planning a return.

Of course, there was no return. I walked the same path again and again, but the garden never reappeared. I walked it as a child, an adolescent, and an adult, always hoping I'd come upon the spot, or that some forces of nature would blend again to recreate the place. But, it never happened.

It may be that garden was not only its own invitation, but its own invention, as well.

Some Things I Learned and When

Terror

    I was four

    The neighborhood kids
    pushed me into a construction hole

        yelled about snakes

        threw stones

wouldn't let me out.

        My mom heard me screaming
        rescued me.

Sin

    Five

    When I crushed
    my baby brother's wafer cone.

    Walking through the shotgun apartment
        saw where he had dropped the cone

    Should I — shouldn't I?

        Left my body

watched the slow motion

foot
          fall

crush — and I knew.

The Long Road of Pleasure

Six — a very good year

Janet Pilkowski
          of the blond and curly locks

in bed — looking at each other's face
                    touching…

the adults were playing cards
auntie walked in
laughed
told the gang

they thought we were cute.

Death

Funeral parlor

My best friend, Richard

Laid out in his

White

Slipping into darkness
        rising up to light

I come to
and realize

      this next breath
      may be

my last

    All's well.

Secret Wings

I had wings
and hovered
high
above
a steel-span
as our family car
dropped
into night.

I kicked my legs
and stretched my wings
in air too thick for flight.

I fell and tumbled
wings and arms
entangled.

Sunlight licked
my eyes
my wings
dissolved.

I stumbled out of bed
as clumsy as any boy
removed from sleep.

I checked outside
my bedroom window—
our family car
squatting
in the drive
as safe as steel.

At breakfast
my mother asked
how I slept.

I frowned
and shrugged
my secret wings.

AN ACT OF CONTRITION

*"In the Sacrament of Penance the penitent is his own accuser,
while the priest acts as judge in the place of Christ."*

The Maryknoll Missal

Seven years old.

The confessional—
dark and quiet

When I kneel
a switch activates
a small bare bulb—
a crude concession
in this ancient rite.

A wooden screen
slides to reveal the mesh window
that separates me from
Jesus in the priest

   This is the way we go to hell...

Bless me, Father
for I have
sinned

  though I didn't know
  until you taught me

This is my
first
confession

Yes, my son?
> seven years old
> trembling before God
> and the voice of this priest
> who I'm sure knows
> who I am

> seven years old
> the age of reason

This is my soul -
an unruled sheet
of white paper
creased lengthwise
and laid flat
fully opened

Look:

"J.M.J"—"Jesus, Mary, Joseph."

faithfully inscribed
and centered on top
for extra credit

and here are the sins of a seven year old

> making fun of my friend
> disobeying my mother

Is there anything else, my son?

> > Emma was the girl next door.

That summer day, hidden under
our dark and stuffy tented blanket
all our senses were awake, our
game was arousal, furtive and
feral.

these are my hands
palms down
angled in
on either side
of the crease
in my soul

Is there anything else?

No, Father.

this is the way
we press on the sheet
this is the way we torque our hands
this is the way the sheet tears

I never told…

right

down

the center.

                              This is the

way…

Make a good

Act of Contrition
and for your
penance…

Oh, my God
I am heartily sorry
for having offended
thee…

Ego te absolvo
a peccatis tuis

I absolve you
of your sins

       This is the way
         we go to hell
            go to hell
               go to hell

    seven years old
    the age of reason
    doomed
    because I never told

        Emma,
        I never told

In nomine Patris
et Filii
et Spiritus Sancti

     but I wished
     I could have

This is the way we go to hell
so early in the morning

Go, and sin no more

Thank you, Father.

DISTRACTING AN ANGEL

Sister told us

Father would be passing
carrying the Viaticum
    grace and abundance
to the sick and dying.

God in his pocket.

She said
not to distract
this Angel of Mercy
by begging for blessings
or tugging at his sleeves —

we were to kneel
or bow our heads

"in silence, in silence."

We were thrilled

but I had to wonder

why

an Angel of Mercy
would cut through
a playground

and not fly directly
to the sad parlors

and bedrooms
of the sick
and dying

and how
any angel
could be
so easily
distracted.

THE ALTAR OF GOD

Introibo ad altare Dei;
ad Deum qui laetificat
juventutem meam.

I go up to the altar of God
the God who gives joy
to my youth.

I wasn't asked
to swing the censer
so never felt the smoky touch
of incense rise past my face
and tendril up to heaven

The hand bells
to raise the din
around the blood and body
were given to
other sinners.

My job was lighting the candles
before the church was filled.

A solo turn
for a stage hand.

The flame reached
from my shame filled heart
through the long brass rod
to ignite the wicks
above the altar

I was sure
my adolescent secrets
were visible to the all-knowing
and burning much brighter
than those tiny flames

I trudged through the rite
a sad
and mumbling angel —
an impostor
in the theater of miracles

until

Ite, missa est
            Go the Mass is over

Wake up, the dream is over

And I would extinguish
the flames

and leave the God

who gave shame
to my youth

to His empty pews
and dark Church.

Go, the Mass is over
            Deo Gratias — thank god

Amen.

IMMORTAL CRUELTY

Twelve years old.

Pennsylvania summer

hot, humid,
bright as sunlight.

Three of us
tramping around
woods and fields
armed with Daisy and
Red Ryder b-b guns
looking for something
easy to kill

and we find it.

A frog
big as a hand
half hidden
near a small stream.

We hush ourselves

stand above it

take aim

and nail it.

It doesn't move,
so the jokes start,

and we pepper it

cock and fire
pump and fire
cock and fire

over and over

intent on our mayhem.

But no matter how close we got,

and we put our barrels
right up to the thing,

the frog didn't move and
none of the pellets penetrated.

At the end of it
the frog looked embossed,
with shiny brass pellets,
rimmed in blood.

We left the croaker
to its misery,
and walked home,
teenagers carrying on
after a little murder.

A minor evil.

A venial sin.

And fifty years later

I'm haunted
by that damn frog,

immortal frog.

Liturgy of the Hours

The prayers
of the day

The Divine Office

Sufficient
as all things
unto the day

I would sit
and watch
my uncle

a catholic priest

read his breviary

the
required
prayers.

A boy
watching
a man
at
prayer

The   The
light   light
around   around
him   them

What was holy

the man
the book
the prayer
the place
the light

the boy watching

All was holy

sufficient

unto the day

sufficient unto eternity.

Seen

"Only a piece of machinery could possibly carry all the world's pain."
—Olga Tokarczuk

The tremendous tires
on the vehicle
that carries
the world's pain
allow it to move

undetected
on
night bound streets.

The driver
of the vehicle
that carries
the world's pain

sits high in his cab

watch-capped

looking
right
then left
then
ahead

checking his mirrors
for any sign
of wandering hurt.

The vehicle
that carries
the world's pain

always full
always
being
filled

is seen
by a boy

pretending
not to be tired

leaning
on a window sill

gazing
through
a
street-light's
aura.

Hello Stranger

I was told
my place
in the universe
while walking
from
motor-pool
to
barracks
on an army base
in Germany

stoned

A joint
rolled in Nam
sealed in an envelope
traveled through the
Army Post Office
and arrived
on my desk

potent

PO-tent

A couple tokes
and I slipped
outside
myself
and
received
a message

while staring
at the sky

I

was
informed
of who

I was

&

where

I

lived.

1966.
The Coleman Kaserne, Gelnhausen, Germany.

A suspicious envelope arrived on my desk. It had no
return address, and appeared to hold nothing but a lump. I
opened it, and the lump was a big, fat joint. I had a pretty
good idea who it was from, but how it got through the
Army postal system without being confiscated, stolen, or
me busted, I had no idea. It may be that all the way down
the line, whoever handled it was just as stoned as I was
about to get. There were a lot of stoners serving in 1966.

I pretended to work late, and allowed some time to pass
after the last person left the office before I locked the
doors, pulled the shades, turned out the lights, and lit
up. I sucked down two hits, and went from nervous to

stoned, zero to sixty, in no time flat.

Those were the days of carbon copies, and onion skin paper. Before long, my desk was covered in pink onion skin and I was agog at the works of man, the play of light, and the wonder of color.

After I came down a little, I straightened out my desk, left, locked the office behind me, and huddled behind an armored personnel carrier where I had one or two more hits before I began the long walk up the hill to Company A barracks.

I was about half-way home when the telegram came, and I was welcomed into the life of all things.

I

spent

the next

twenty years

chasing

that

one

high.

THE SKIDS

1966
The Village

I was more alone, and more depressed than I knew alone
and depressed could be so I followed my heroes to the
skids.

I didn't know if I was a tourist seeing the sights, or a
sight being seen.

Skids run down hill, and though the bottom looks a long
way off, whatever cart you're in

    alcohol

    drugs

    alcohol & drugs

    sex

    the thrills & chills of crime and remorse

could be run off the track, bunging up the ride, and
way-stationing you at some bottom that wasn't true
bottom, but true enough.

Time on the skids passes in ripples. Time submerged.

Wake up in a pay-by-the-day SRO, light from an air
shaft, time told in sweat and sheets, and it's time to move,
oh so slow, to some place where I can sink black, where

I know nobody, nobody knows me, and everybody is a
mendicant

begging and trading whatever they have for as much as
could be got

and I'm trading my young body for

a shot
and a beer

and a shot
and a beer

hit me again and take me home to your bare bulb flop

a shot
and a beer

and touch me

I'm lonely

and pay me - money

or buy me something to eat

and pay me

I'm alone.

Wake up, time is sunlight turning everything to angles
sharp as blue blades

light blind and still alone more alone
looking for another ride down

to where I thought I wanted to be

hoping I'd die before I killed myself.

1969/Dancers

We loved our bodies
    what they could do
        what we could do
           with them.

Radiant

Shapely

Perfected
    in heat
       and
    provocation

Making prayers
    from rude animal energy.

We loved our bodies

Quiet as sand
    nestled
        grain to grain

Settled
    into shapes

Graceful
    as dusk
        and dunes.

My Celestial Bodies

The angel of secrets

The angel of forgotten dreams

The angel of sleep and repose

Tomorrow's angel

The angel of delight and pain — an archangel

The heart's angel

Graveside angels

A snow angel at the center of a pine grove — no footprints to or fro

The angel in the schoolyard

The angel of desire and despair — some say a fiend

The angel above the fiesta — watching out for the borrachos and the foolish girls

Casino angel — the angel of dumb luck

The angel of speech — the mutterers and stutterers angel

The angel of the sewers — St. Ignatz of the Rats

The angel of numbers and signs

Languid angels

Pool hall angels

The angel at the river's end

The angel in the bamboo forest

Nursing home angel

The angels of battle

The angel of good counsel

The angel at the Gates of Eden

Angels in free fall

The necessary angels —

Angels watchin' over me, my Lord.

FIELD NOTES

ALL LIFE — ALL LIVING

for Reggie

All life has voice and sings of itself
A great and resounding song of itself
The choir of life sings "Life!"

Wind and the River
Rain and the Sun
Have voice
And are alive!

The Flowers and the Clover and the Dirt
Have voice
Sing life
And are alive!

Even the Rocks have voice
Sing songs so low and down
Deep in a rumble
And close to the ground
Sing life
And are alive!

And the Sky has a voice
Sings blue
Sings gray
Sings cloud
And the Clouds sing cloud
Sing life
And are alive!

The Child and the Man
The Woman and the Child

The two footed
Four footed
Many footed
No footed
Sing
And are Alive!

And the Dust
And the Bones
In the grave
Have a voice
And Death
Has a voice
A whisper and a rattle of life
Takes life, gives life
And is
Alive!

All life has voice and sings of itself
A great and resounding song of itself

The Choir of Life

Sings!

God's Beautiful Rain Body

In Seattle

God's beautiful

Rain body

Covers us over

And our home

Is a boat

Afloat

On a sea

Of grass and flowers.

Lavatera

Sprays up

Against our kitchen window.

Dahlias bob

In the breeze.

Squash

Blossoms

Into starfish.

And day lilies

Buoy and beacon

Against the back fence.

In this ocean

Of planted motion

Thoughts rise

And become

Spirit-Fish,

All neon — dart — and flash,

And wonder

Is luminous.

ENTRANCEMENT

When a forest enters your dream

You feel

roots groaning
toward water
and leaves
brushing
sky.

When a mountain enters your dream

You feel
every stone
trembling
on its slope

When crow enters

You balance

on thin branches
tasting breezes
from the north.

All the mad chemical jokes
your brain tells itself
are nothing

when wind enters your dream
and you ride rough currents
ecstatic & wild

Until as always

dreams go to ground

daylight slips
across your face

your eyelids flutter

and you beg
your anxious animals

for just a little more sleep.

Field Notes
02.02.2019
Cerro Pelon – Macheros *(the Mexico/Michoacán border)*

1.

I'm lying on a soft century
of pine needles

Air dusted with sun-shot orange

Monarchs
clustered
in tall pines

> drop
> flutter
> glide

A million wings—
a subtle and holy thrum.

2.

A river of butterflies
roll & tumble
down green corridors

A celebration of saints
dance their way
past outstretched arms
to a sunlit field.

3.

Dress me in butterflies
Cover me in butterflies
Comfort me with butterflies

My eyes
my eyes
filled with butterflies

Bury me
when you bury me
in the midst
of butterflies.

I Open My Heart

and the world walks in

shattered battered illumined

filthy tattered bloody begging

Saints in various ways

these are my guests and my teachers

the loves of my life and the terrors

Let's set the table

&

enjoy the party.

Field Notes
07.04.2019
Seattle @ 939

At 3:15

the breeze
returns

trees
resume
their
songs
&
elocutions

bees
come
to
blue catnip

two
white moths
jitterbug
across
the
lawn.

Field Notes
07.06.2019
Seattle, 25th & Union

Hungry Water

Strolling past
like Christ on a Crutch

Everything he owns
cloaking his battered-ness
or in a shopping cart

My greeting is
a baited hook in
hungry water

Reverse fishing
make the cast
become the catch

No current strong enough
to allay, "can you spare…"

I can and so I do
with smile and eyes

and see:

in harsh light
and stark reality

that none of us
are free.

This is Us

for Reggie

hummingbird & dog

You, with your 500
   heartbeats thrumming
      every minute

Me, with a lub dub
   steady as
      deep sleep

You, all enthusiasm
   for the next person
      next thing
   movement and moment

Me, loyal and grateful
   stomping down a circle or
      looking
      for something
         to eat.

This is us
   still in love

hummingbird & dog

   all these years.

Happy Valentine's Day, Seattle – 2012
arf!

Unexpected Love /
Sweet Coincidence

for Eddie and Kate

Yesterday, I saw
an old friend
and surprised myself
by kissing his hand.

Unexpected love.

Today, I saw
a different friend
and she
surprised me
in the same way.

Sweet coincidence.

A Short History, Beginning to End

1.

~~God~~
in all
~~God's~~
glory

Explosive

ragged

aflame

A raging expansion

extending and delineating

Everything.

2.

Human Beings
came lumbering
onto the scene
baring our teeth
and scratching
at parasites

&

Here we are
straddling cyberspace

baring our teeth
and scratching.

3.

Bloody Century—the 20th

Red ants
living
in a
red ant hill
given the gift of fire

we burnt
some cities
to a crisp

and all the people
in them.

4.

Lumbering we were
and lumbering still
we crashed the 21st
turned the jets up high
and ruined dinner for everyone

Then we left the kitchen
with the oven on.

5.

Billionaires in rocket ships
where they gonna' run to?

~~God~~
in all
~~God's~~
glory

mouth
wide

swallows a fly

Perhaps
we'll
die.

Field Notes/Quick Sketch
01.03.2020
Plaza Mexiamora, Guanajuato

Cool morning
sunshine

reflected warmth from cobbles and metal benches

pigeons gathered—dirty birds doing no harm looking
for scraps but the kids who usually eat lunch here are on
break so no drips dribbles drops or discards to be had

three dogs small to large waiting in line one after the
other to piss on the same doorpost smallest dog lives
there pees first then last.

Two-leggeds going about their business carrying
garrafones of water and tanks of gas through ridiculously
small doorways; crossing the plaza with fifty pound bags
of cement on their backs, or multiple cases of coca-cola.
Human burros where no cars can come and wheelbarrows
and dollies are after thoughts or just too much a pain.

Yellow leaves making scuttle sounds cluster up in corners
and against curbs.

What is it about our species that in wanting more – no
matter how much we have—we're willing to kill each
other in order to grasp and destroy what little remains?
For grandma at the trash one more aluminum can may
be the prize—for certain American families another
twenty-five million greenbacks.

We've just killed two killers. The markets like it. My retirement is momentarily more secure.

The world is burning at the rate of a half-a-billion dead animals.

In Mexiamora, the cat is belled, seems to know it, and walks right through the gathered pigeons without a sideways glance and the birds don't even stir just keep pecking for nothing.

Time to move on; feel my face aging in the sun.

Somos el Barco

We are the boat

supple
&
seaworthy

hollow
&
solid

capable of journeys
as far as time.

Our holds
are filled
with treasure

we have been
merciless
in our
acquisition.

Somos el Mar

We are the sea

waves
&
shoals

whirlpools

currents
&
dangers

we
are
the
storms
upon
the
ocean.

What frightens us
we call wilderness

what we don't understand
we call treacherous

we are

wild
&
treacherous.

We are the sea

we are the boat

we are the people.

FIELD NOTES
03.01.2019
THURGOOD MARSHALL PLAYGROUND, SEATTLE

Eight year old girl
in Seattle black leggings and top
with turquoise wrap-arounds

long hair

running

arms outstretched

knolls & slopes

laughing

as she lifts off

into

Original Joy

(Happy landings, kid.)

At Natan's Bar Mitzvah

for the Lee-Engle mishpooka

Alone
with
the
eternal

the
eternal
asks
nothing

loving-kindness
arises
from
an
experienced
heart

travels
tatter-winged
through
our
lives

even/especially
with
the
most wounded
of us.

FIELD NOTES
DELHI, INDIA — 2001
Dedicated to my buddy, Rajiv Gupta

WATER

As gift and greeting

to my Western sensibility
not rare or precious
just – water

to my hosts
as central to their lives
as if they lived
on the planet Dune

to my Western sensibility

we were on
the planet Dune

Delhi – 2001

ninety degrees F.
humidity off the charts
air relatively clear
not yet the gas chamber
it would become.

Rajiv has brought me
to meet a real-estate broker

We're standing on the downward slope

of a lawn that rolls like a green wave
from the broker's office door

Water

as gift and greeting

delivered by a servant
carried on a silver tray
held in tall and sweating glasses

Rajiv and I are corporate cas(ual)

broker and servant are trad(itional)
in white khurta and pajama sets

a procession of two with the servant leading

with the water -
leading

imagination might summon
elephants and parasols.

The water is offered
and though I'm as hot and humid as Delhi
I hesitate and find myself on the spot

Looks are exchanged

I run the math of
need health hospitality and custom

a moment of disassociation

phantom cameras whirring

one of those dramatic crane shots

of four players
diminished in size
on a ridiculously green
and well-watered lawn

I accept the water
re-enter my body
our tiny world exhales

business begins.

Tips passed
fees negotiated
addresses exchanged

we return our glasses
to the servant's silver tray
and shake hands in that gentle Indian way

ritual
test
and business

blest and complete

contract written

in water.

Delhi is a dune city built on sand and rock. The population in 2001 was about thirteen million, as of this writing it is nearer twenty-eight million.

When the population was a mere seventeen million, forty-six percent of those had no access to piped water. Water is politically allocated. Middle and upper class cantonments have greater access to clean water than the majority of the population. Even so, scarcity is an issue.

Many of my co-workers were forced to rise at four a.m., to wait for water trucks so they could get their families' daily allotment.

"If you like the oil wars, you're going to love the water wars."— Zack Works

The broker's tip did lead to a fabulous sublet in Gurgoun, a.k.a., electronic city. Rajiv informed me there was no way we were paying a fee for a mere "tip."

FOR BOBBY LESSER

Remember that two dollar bill you gave me
with the dime taped to it?

I'd been wondering for awhile
how to pass it along.

Joey almost got it a couple times —
as a love gift — the way I got it.

Tonight a young guy tossed a two dollar bill
into the basket. Said it was the last of his money.

I grabbed him after, and gave him our two dollar bill
with the dime taped to it.

Said, see that, you came out ahead.

I knew that bill wasn't going to stay
in my wallet forever.

Field Notes
06.15.2015
Lopez Island, Washington

Eagle

eyed in the
cool blue
circles slow
watching for
some
dumb
bunny
to forget
time of day
&
stray
from
blackberry bramble
to
tender shoots.

Fur wrapped
too cute
pound of flesh

twitches

and hops...

SHELTER IN PLACE

In the shelter
shelter of a thought

In the shelter
of a gaze

Who watches?

In the shelter
shelter of your arms

In the shelter
of your heart

Who watches?

In the shelter
rooms & shadows

In the shelter
doorways
alleys

Who watches
watches over you?

In the shelter
words & phrases

In the shelter
silence
breath

In the shelter
life & death

Who watches
who watches
who watches
over you?

Coda:

EVERYTHING

is held

even

emptiness

is

contained.

THE THROAT OF THUNDER

How

how do we
how do we rise
how do we rise above
how do we rise above the heartbreak
how do we rise above the heartbreak of being
     of being
     of being
     alive
how do we rise above the heartbreak of being alive?

  I lift my eyes
     to the great sky

  Shift my gaze
     to the world of wonder

Listen to the rain

Listen to the throat of thunder.

Harvest Spinning

There are countries where the terminally ill sell their bones and body parts to be collected after death. The parts are purchased from the harvesters by medical schools and collectors.

The family eats; the rent is paid; Monsanto gets its cut.

This is not a pawn, not a loan. No tickets or i.o.u.'s are issued or signed. There is no redemption, only collection.

Sometimes, before the body's last breath, the collectors arrive and man-handle the soon to be or not to be out to the jungle, alley, basement, warehouse bathtub for a careful harvest of bones and parts.

The money doesn't last.

Spinning

wife gone spinning

spinning

money gone spinning

spinning

wife gone spinning

spinning

money gone spinning
rent not paid
spinning

money gone spinning

shame

wife gone spinning

spinning

wife gone spinning

spinning

spinning from the spinning

ceiling fan.

FEAR

I dreamed I stabbed a deer and laid it on its side.
It spoke to me and did not die.

FEARS
return
over & again

close the door
they seep
across the threshold

seal the windows
they find their way
as drafts

spray all the repellent
our wizards can devise
and they will dress themselves
from your closet

ignore them
and they will pester
your sleep.

Open your arms

watch them
step forward stumble back
unsure of the tune
you've called

Set the table

and they will
gorge themselves
into
skeletons
and
smoke

Breathe easy

the wind
will
carry
them
away

I dreamed I stabbed a deer
and laid it on its side

It spoke to me, and did not die.

Entrances to Hell

Sources tell us there are either eleven or thirteen.

Sources are wrong.

As wrong
as the number
of the number
of rivers on earth

How many rivers are on earth?

Answer: Nobody knows how many rivers are on earth.

By the way, we know there is one invisible river, the Sarasvati, which leads us to wonder how many other invisible rivers there may be.

Answer: nobody knows. They're invisible.

Try
counting
the
number
of
people
on
earth

Answer: 7,714,526,923
        (give or take)

        And that is how many entrances there are
        to hell (give or take.)

Us

We are too full of ourselves

    to be comfortable

    with

        buzzards watching for death

        crows making tools for theft

        coyotes thriving everywhere.

Our animal nature

    mammal life

scares the hell out of us
so we see ourselves made
in a dead god's image

somewhere above

            our fur-bearing
            breast sucking
            shit producing

                selves.

But

our footprints carry a scent

and mortality is on our trail

       just over there

with the buzzards
and the crows
and the coyotes.

THIS IS THE DAY

for my good dog Sammy

This is the day,
simple and sure.

Clouds slip over the sun
and off again.

Steady wheel–whoosh of traffic.

I nurse a cup of coffee
at a sidewalk cafe
with my good dog Sammy
asleep next to the table.

A pigeon makes its pigeon-way to lunch down the street.

A beautiful East African girl
        bundled against the cold
slips around Sam
        hands me a pamphlet
and asks

Do you know for sure if you died today that you would
go to heaven?

And I say

Yes,

because I'm already there.

Scars

for Jennifer Kay Hamann, a.k.a. SmashFaceKid

i.

If I could weave
all my scars
and wear them
as a mask

Would people say
they'd seen
the real me
at last?

ii.

I'm looking
at a jagged
eight inch scar
down my right knee

rough

surgeon went in twice

turns white
under sun tan

looks like
nothing
but
a
scar.

I'm looking
at the four inch doozy
on my left wrist

nothing
but
a
scar.

Same with the nick
on my chin

six inchers on my abdomen
right foot right arm.

Wound anything

body
soul
land-scape

leave a scar.

It's a sign
you've healed

sure — and

it's a reminder
you've been hurt.

Old wounds

old scars
no pain
constant reminders.

To Alter and Adorn

1.

For years, now, I've been secretly admiring the fashion
sense of the 8 – 12 year old set. Today, I'm wearing black
and white shoes, striped socks, green pants, a cranberry
hoodie, and a baby blue watch cap. But, there's another
guy, about my age, a few rows down who's all orange with
stripes and glitter. Damn! If I could only find a silver cape.

2.

The impulse
is toward
expansion
until
fear
is taught.

Then we
contract

and are controlled.

3.

Bonsai, topiary, lawns
trimmed into art
yearning for the wild
and then:

the trauma
of the ruminants.

This is My Body

This is my venerable
and ancient body

This is my nearsighted
pot-bellied body

This is my chip toothed
bent and trembling body

This is my body
of broken bones and scars

This is my body
and because you love me
this is my body
made beautiful
by your beautiful body.

Gratitude Always Leads to God

Just not the one you're thinking of

not the meddler—

the Immensity.

Departure

Sorrow
born of loss

Loss
the truth
of everything

Knowing this —
freedom.

Death arrives
and discovers
there's nothing
to steal

You depart
on a breath.

All Across America Buddhas Sit

All

across

America

Buddha

(s)

sit

(s)

ALL ACROSS AMERICA BUDDHAS SIT

FUN WITH DICK AND JANE

Self shifts
with each
person
I
see

I
am no more
my self
to you
than
I
am

to

me.

A room full of you
looking at me
see

who you think

you

see.

I
am

me

until

I am

an other
me

which is
another me

which
is
an
other

which
is

which…

?

Bowing

to this world

To the quiet
that will never be silence

Bowing to trees
surrounding

Bowing to space
above

Bowing to stars
masked by daylight

Bowing to honor
our great star

Bowing toward
the infinite
eternity

Bowing to honor
your soul's journey

Bowing to honor
my own soul's journey

Bowing to acknowledge
the reaper of souls

Bowing in gratitude

Bowing.

SWEET
for Coach Tricia Arcaro Turten

Mornings

When I'm through
at the gym

Having punched
in, out, and around
air, moments, and people

I shower
change and
walk the street

sharp

like a razor
slicing paper

Clean.

(O.G.)

Dust unto Dust

1.

Dust unto dust
has always
left me wondering
who might be
suspended
in that shaft
of light
angling
through
the window.

Moses, Caesar,
my old friend, Marie;

A galaxy of souls?

I pass my hand
through the gathering
disturb
the dance
and
some
motes
cling.

2.

When
Jesus
and his mother
left,

it's said
they left
completely,

body & soul.

We may breathe
the same air,
but we're not
the same dust.

3.

When I was a boy
I hated getting
my hands dirty,

I'd wash them
in the middle
of whatever
I was doing.

As an adult
I still can't stand
dirty hands.

I won't garden,
dirt under my nails
drives me crazy.

Into dust,
you say?

How will I ever
stand myself?

LAMENT
for Phebe Jewell

Trouble

and I can't drag
two-hundred bucks
outta my bank account

What bank account

and I can't drag
a hundred bucks
outta the old man's bank account

What bank account

and I can't drag
fifty bucks outta my
best friend's bank account

What best friend

Trouble

is not my middle name

my middle name is
busted
my last name is
broke
and my first name is
flat

Flat god-damn Busted Broke

And ain't life just grand
in Donald Trump's America
        which is
            America the Same

        24/7
all the time
doesn't matter
who's squatting
in the White House
        Ain't my house

It is
        my America

        every 50 states of it
            and territories
                like Samoa

        and I resent
        that with all this real-estate

I can't drag
two-hundred bucks
outta my non-existent
bank account.

RESURRECTION SHOWER

After months
flat on my back
restricted to bed-baths
I began my return.

The first day of Ramadan

in a nursing home

in a wheel chair

under a shower

with a tender
Muslim aide
aiming the spray
of hot water
onto my head.

Pleasure
so intense
I saw stars

and shivered
and laughed
and shouted

Thank God!

And that aide lit up

joined my glee

ran
a washcloth
across my chest

and whispered

Al-Hamdu Lillah.

At the PCC
(The Beauty of Age)

I'm walking
through the co-op
singing

Singing at the PCC

Walking through the veggies singing
singing to the veggies
sleepy veggies
walking through the veggies singing

Walking though the PCC

singing to the oats
singing to the cheese
singing to the coffee
louder for the coffee
singing for the coffee
singing

On to the fish
glassy eyed fish
sing my saddest
for the poor dead fish
deep-sea sounds
for the poor dead fish

Over to the pastry singing
sing sweet songs
do a little dance
for the pastry—yes
Yes

the beauty of age

I am happy to be
and if all I am is happy to be
I'm happy to be
an old man singing
at the PCC.

*PCC *– Puget Consumers' Co-Op*

5/20

He sits
hears a breeze
pleasing
sweet.

Cocks his head
feels the breeze
across his lips
cool.

Removes his hat
beads of sweat
catch the light
shine like jewels.

Sweat
breeze
light
jewels

gone

and still

he sits

he sits still.

To Be

for Greta Thunberg

Doctors of our lives

We would focus our fierce intelligence
on the only balm for our fearful existence —

> Love
> for all
> creation.

We would find
our daily dose
of good sense to offset
the nonsense

> merchants
> power-mad
> &
> false-do-gooders

> peddle

where e'er we roam.

We would have eyes to see

> blue sky
> quarter moon
> beautiful dream morning.

Each moment passing

precious.

OUTSIDE

winter's
sharp
light

inside

the
extravagance
of a tulip

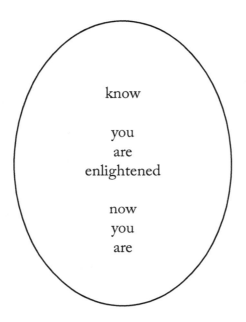

know

you
are
enlightened

now
you
are